YOUR BEST LIFE SERIES

How to Create Your
MEANINGFUL MISSION

Live Your Life with More Purpose,
Passion and Commitment

MICHAEL E. ANGIER

Published by Success Networks International, Inc.
Tampa Bay, Florida 34609-9509

www.SuccessNet.org

ISBN: 9781695416680
© Copyright 2019
All Rights Reserved

Limit of Liability/Disclaimer of Warranty

While the author and publisher have used their best efforts in preparing this book, they make no representation or warranties with respect to the accuracy or completeness of the contents and specifically disclaim any implied warranties. You should consult with a professional where appropriate. The author or publisher shall not be liable for any loss of profit or any other commercial damages, including but not limited to special, incidental, consequential or other damages.

Early Reviews

"*How to Create Your Meaningful Mission* should be standard issue for anyone starting out or beginning a new phase of life. The author builds the case for having personal, family, organizational and corporate mission statements—and then shows us step by step how to do it. The book has great examples and even covers the challenges and pitfalls to avoid or overcome. Five stars, for sure."

—Susan McGrogan
www.CodingServicesGroup.com

"*The topic of developing a Meaningful Mission Statement is one that more people in our communities could benefit from today. I especially like the key steps laid out in Chapter 5 to get your mission statement started. These steps can act as a filter to help improve or revise your current mission statement. The concise presentation of this work could help you draft your statement over a weekend, as Michael mentions. The key is to get started with the framework to see what comes from within you and gets expressed onto your paper.*"

—Shane Fielder
www.SamuraiInnovation.com

This Book is for You if You...

- want to maximize your time, energy and effort in a worthwhile cause—*your best life!*
- aren't satisfied with an average life—you want something bigger and better than that.
- want greater clarity for the path your life takes.
- desire to create a legacy—an exceptional life of meaning and significance—one that truly matters.
- are committed to creating a mission based upon your core values, strongly held beliefs and empowering purpose.
- desire to think bigger and believe in the possibilities of living up to your full and unique potential.
- want to believe more in yourself and in what's possible.
- want to learn about resources and recommendations that will help you create a clear and Meaningful Mission for living your Best Life.
- have a desire to dig deeper, think more comprehensively and live in a more balanced, meaningful and significant fashion.

Even if You...

- already have a mission statement but want to make it bigger, better and more inspiring.
- are a teenager or have already entered your Golden Years.
- think your life is great and can't get any better.

Table of Contents

Introduction 1

Chapter 1: Your Best Life 3

Chapter 2: Mission Defined 11

Chapter 3: Why Your Mission Matters 15

Chapter 4: Preparing to Write Your Mission Statement 19

Chapter 5: Drafting Your Mission Statement 21

Chapter 6: Mission Statement Examples 27

Chapter 7: Refining Your Mission Statement 31

Chapter 8: Organizational Mission Statements 33

Chapter 9: Other Mission Statements 39

Chapter 10: Overcoming Challenges to Your Mission 41

Chapter 11: The Path to Your Best Life 45

Chapter 12: In Summary 47

A Thank You and a Request 50

About the Author 51

Other Books by Michael Angier 54

Free Resources 58

Acknowledgements 59

Introduction

> *"Every person above the ordinary has a certain mission that they are called to fulfill."*
> —Johann Wolfgang von Goethe

I wrote this book to help you discover, develop, define and refine your own personal magnetic, magnificent Meaningful Mission.

This book (and the entire *Your Best Life* series) is dedicated to helping you live your very best life (see Chapter One for Best Life definition).

When I work with people on their core values, their purpose, mission and vision, I think of myself as walking on hallowed ground. I consider these foundational building blocks sacred because I know they transform lives. I don't approach this work lightly.

What is Your Mission?

A mission statement represents your belief system—the priorities, values and principles that measure your decisions. It provides overall direction and clarifies your purpose and meaning.

Michael E. Angier

When you clearly know what you want to be and to do in your life, you feel strong in your sense of mission. You're no longer driven by everything that happens to you. Rather, you feel a deep and complete commitment to following your innermost values.

And you're excited by it! People sense your strength and direction—you become a powerful, positive decision maker—in your professional and personal life.

This book is primarily for someone who does not currently have a mission. But it can also be useful for someone who has a mission and wants to check in on its clarity, focus and direction—to polish it up a bit, refine it, expand it or even create a new one.

You are Never Too Old

Many people think they are too old to claim a mission for themselves. That's just not true.

Having a Meaningful Mission earlier in your life might have been better, but no one can change the past—not even God!

Whether you are 19 or 90, it's never too late to work through the process I will set forth for you. Very few people know how much time they have left on this planet. Clarity on your Meaningful Mission and conviction in its pursuit will make the *rest* of your life the *best* of your life. It will put life in your years and not simply years in your life.

Are you excited to create your Meaningful Mission—or deepen the one you think you have? I am. Let's get to it.

Chapter 1:
Your Best Life

"Decide what kind of life you really want . . . And then, say no to everything that isn't that."

Are You Seeking Your Best Life?

Before we get into the nitty gritty of developing your meaningful mission, let's take a look at our objectives.

If you're reading this, I assume you want a better life. You want to improve on where you are. Maybe a little. Maybe a lot.

Regardless of where you find yourself at this point in time—and regardless of your age—you can certainly improve. After all, the biggest room in the world is the room for improvement.

You may be wanting to take your already on-purpose, comfortable life and simply make it better.

Or maybe your life is a train wreck.

Either way, you have to start with the end in mind.

Michael E. Angier

It's important to acknowledge where you are, but there will be plenty of time for that. What's more important is getting clear on where you're going.

Your best life doesn't just happen. It doesn't automatically unfold, and it's certainly not handed to you. You have to design and create your best life yourself. Because if you don't, other people and outside circumstances will do it for you. And do you know what other people and outside circumstances have planned for you? Hardly anything at all.

What Does Your Best Life Look Like?

No doubt you have some idea about what your Best Life looks like. I assume you have some goals—some things you want to accomplish or experience before you make your departure from planet Earth.

Have you ever envisioned, in great detail, how you would like to have your life unfold? Do you see it? Can you taste it? Do you believe it? Can you imagine how it feels?

The clearer you can become on all the things you want in your life—and the reasons why—the easier it will be to do what you need to do to achieve them.

We all want to be happy, and I personally believe we are happiest when we are in pursuit of our highest and best.

For now, let me share with you, in general terms, what I mean by your Best Life. It should give you some seminal ideas for your Best Life Plan.

How to Create Your Meaningful Mission

It's a tall order, but I think your Best Life is a life without regrets.

> *"Your Best Life is a life without regrets."*

Your Best Life is a life by design—not default.

I think you should build a life from which you don't need a vacation. Not that you won't *take* vacations, but you won't *need* them. Because your vocation will be your avocation. And it's not a struggle; it's a wiggle.

Your Best Life requires your best self. If you want your life to get better, *you* have to get better. I'm guessing that's why you're reading this book.

> *"Your Best Life requires your best self."*

For me it means rising to a calling instead of an alarm clock. I get up when I *want* to get up, and I use an alarm clock only once or twice a year. It is possible.

I believe your Best Life is a life of clarity, purpose, passion and prosperity. A life designed around your values, principles and intentions.

Simply put—a life on your terms. You get to design, define, create and live Your Best Life.

Michael E. Angier

Top Seven Results of Living Your Best Life

The following seven benefits are what I consider the biggest payoffs for creating a life well lived.

1. Significance & Meaning
2. Time, Location & Financial Freedom
3. Happiness, Fun & Adventure
4. Purpose & Integrity
5. Confidence & Self-esteem
6. Rich Relationships
7. Health, Fitness & Vitality

Sounds worthwhile, yes?

Your full and unique potential is unknown. But certainly worth going for, don't you think? Who can count the number of apples in a single apple seed?

> *"Death is not the greatest loss in life. The greatest loss is what dies inside us while we live."*
> —Norman Cousins

The Path to Your Best Life

The illustration below shows what I see as the best path to your best life—however you might define it. The bottom four tiers are foundational. The top three are much more dynamic. But they should stand in support of your core values, purpose, mission and vision.

The Path to Your Best Life

Anything, Not Everything

My belief is that you can do *anything* in this life. But you can't do *everything*. That's why it's so important to choose your goals, your projects and your tasks wisely. And to base them on the foundational steps of your core values, purpose, mission and vision.

Michael E. Angier

> *"You can do* anything *you want in this life. You just can't do* everything *you want."*

Otherwise, you're making choices and spending your precious time and energy on your own or others' whims.

The first foundational step (Core Values) is not within the scope of this book, but I strongly encourage you to think carefully about them. Getting clear on your core values, your purpose and your mission will help you to avoid regrets and feel that you invested your life in the best way possible.

Although you can develop your meaningful mission without a clear sense of your most important core values, you will find it easier, and most likely a much more empowering and effective purpose, if you know your top core values.

SuccessNet has an inexpensive course you can use to go through this process. It's a home-study course that's available in print form as well as an online video course at no additional cost. You can access a discounted price on the Your Core Values Course at www.YourCoreValues.com

> *"Life should not be a journey to the grave with the intention of arriving safely in a pretty and well-preserved body, but rather to skid in broadside in a cloud of smoke, thoroughly used up, totally worn out, and loudly proclaiming 'Wow, what a ride!'"*
> —Hunter S. Thompson

The bottom line is that unless you invest the time, energy and money in creating a life you truly want, you're going to be spending a lot of time and effort supporting a life you *don't* want.

> *"Unless you invest the time, energy and money in creating a life you truly want, you're going to be spending a lot of time and effort supporting a life you don't want."*

Michael E. Angier

Action Steps

Please consider this engaging and inspiring home-study video course on discovering and clarifying your core values. To find out more, go to www.YourCoreValues.com

It's nominally priced. Thousands of people have taken this course and are living more purpose-driven lives because of the process.

Chapter 2:
Mission Defined

> *"Outstanding people have one thing in common: An absolute sense of mission."*
> —Zig Ziglar

You may have heard other speakers, authors and trainers talking about mission, vision and purpose as if they were the same thing. I don't see it that way.

Up until recently, I used purpose and mission interchangeably. But when I started writing a book on the subject, I realized they were not the same. That's why this book is about a Meaningful Mission, and there's another one called *Discover Your Empowering Purpose*.

Your purpose is your reason for being—your raison d'être. It's deeper—more personal. It's what you were meant to do. It may even have existed before you were born. And it's to be discovered rather than selected. Your core values are about who you are.

Your mission is how you show up in the world. It's the vehicle you use to create your vision.

Your Meaningful Mission is more of a direction that you choose for your life. It's the way you *fulfill* your purpose.

Michael E. Angier

Your mission may be one you have your entire life. It could change, and that's OK. But it's bigger than a change in careers—that's more of a strategy.

Wikipedia defines a mission statement as: "A statement of purpose for a company, organization or person, its reason for existing. The mission statement should guide the actions of the organization, spell out its overall goal, provide a path, and guide decision-making. It provides the framework or context within which the company's strategies are formulated. It's like a goal for what the company wants to do for the world."

Your mission is the way you create value in the world. Our fulfillment doesn't come from *getting*, it comes from giving, contributing, adding more value. The more you give, the more fulfilled you are.

A mission statement is a declaration that motivates and inspires you to stay the course. It provides guidance and helps you have more courage when you are confronted with challenges.

How will you change the world? What will be your contribution to the world? How will you serve? Because one person can and does make a difference. Mahatma Gandhi said, "A small body of determined spirits fired by an unquenchable faith in their mission can alter the course of history."

How to Create Your Meaningful Mission

> *"A small body of determined spirits fired by an unquenchable faith in their mission can alter the course of history."*
> —Mahatma Gandhi

Creating your Meaningful Mission is part detection, discovery and exploration. *And* part creation, invention and choosing.

It's also not something you think you *should* do. It has to be what *you* want, not what you think you should want.

Having a clear mission allows you to live a life in support of your core values and your purpose.

Action Step

I challenge you to commit to following through with this process. Your Best Life is worth it. It's not easy, but it is worth it. I promise. Affirm to yourself now: "I promise to complete this book and this process of creating my Meaningful Mission and live my life with more purpose, passion, direction and commitment."

The next chapter will address why it matters.

Michael E. Angier

Chapter 3:
Why Your Mission Matters

"The most effective way to begin with the end in mind is to develop a mission statement."
—Stephen Covey

This is your life. No one else's. No doubt you have roles to play and responsibilities to others, but no one else runs your life. Things happen that affect you, but you choose your response to those events. You are 100 percent responsible for your life. It's up to you to make the best of it.

And that starts with choosing your path, your Meaningful Mission. There is nothing you have to do in this world except for a few body functions—like breathing. You have choice. Sometimes it doesn't feel like we have that much choice, but we do.

Having your Meaningful Mission will make all your decisions easier. When faced with choices—which we all are—you can make choices that best support your mission. You will be less likely to be chasing off after bright and shiny things that only distract you from your mission.

Michael E. Angier

I think you should take your life very seriously. Not in a grim way, not heavy, not negatively—but seriously. You have one life to live, and I think you should look upon it as sacred and precious.

And that's why it's so important to make considered, thoughtful and deliberate choices in crafting your Meaningful Mission.

Without it you can wander from goal to goal, sometimes aimless, sometimes driven—but not always toward your highest and best. Without a clear mission you can never expect to achieve your full and unique potential.

I believe you can be happy doing your best each day at whatever you might be doing—enjoying the precious present and being grateful for what you have. But to be fully actualized, to feel truly fulfilled, and exceptionally satisfied, you must live your best life.

And having an empowering purpose and a clear Meaningful Mission guiding you—leading you—is the surest way I know of to achieving that.

It enables you to gain something beyond what fleeting pleasures can provide.

Meaningfulness. Significance. Value. To feel that you've made a difference in the world and that your life truly mattered. Isn't this what you want?

And you *can* make a difference. I love what Gandhi said, "In a gentle way, you can shake the world."

How to Create Your Meaningful Mission

A meaningful Mission is the vehicle, the guiding light, the way to that end.

> *"In a gentle way, you can shake the world."*
> —Mahatma Gandhi

Action Step

Acknowledge yourself for taking on this most important work of creating your Meaningful Mission. Most people don't. You are. Pat yourself on the back. And please accept my genuine respect and congratulations.

Michael E. Angier

Chapter 4:
Preparing to Write Your Mission Statement

"Before anything else, preparation is the key to success."
—Alexander Graham Bell

I'm sure you're anxious to get started crafting your Meaningful Mission, but don't start writing a mission statement without first *preparing* to write it.

You may come up with it quickly—over a weekend perhaps. But it could also take some time. And it's *worth* the time. It's worth the effort, the thinking, the brainstorming, the introspection. Remember, it's your *life!*

Stephen Covey, the author of *7 Habits of Highly Effective People* (highly recommended) wrote, "A mission statement is not something you write overnight. But fundamentally, your mission statement becomes your constitution, the solid expression of your vision and values. It becomes the criterion by which you measure everything else in your life."

And only you can do this. It can't be farmed out or delegated. No one else on the planet can do this for you.

Michael E. Angier

Studies have shown that only about three percent of Americans have clearly stated and written goals. And I would guess that the percentage of people with a personal mission statement is even smaller than the three percenters. So congratulations on being willing to become part of this elite minority.

I suggest that you block out some time that you will not be easily interrupted or distracted. Expect to do some deep thinking. From what I see, very few people have much thinking time. We have thoughts, for sure. But having thoughts is not real thinking. Real thinking is asking tough questions. It involves clarifying problems and brainstorming and creating solutions. It often means making tough choices. Remember you can do anything, but not *everything*.

Action Steps

Find a comfortable place to start this process. Block out the time, turn off the phone, ask not to be interrupted, and have something to write with and on.

This solitude will help you get in touch with what matters most to you. Without interruptions, you can become introspective and ask yourself a series of questions to help you gather information about your values, priorities and direction.

Chapter 5:
Drafting Your Mission Statement

> *"Two roads diverged in a wood—and I, I took the one less traveled by, and that has made all the difference."*
> —Robert Frost

As I mentioned earlier, this process is part discovery and part creation. You get to choose it. But it's never helpful to force it. You don't want to "push the river". It will eventually flow from you. You will know it when you have it. You'll feel it.

Here are some exercises that will help you get in touch with the various elements of your Meaningful Mission:

1. What Brings You Joy?

Make a list of 50 things that brought you great joy in the past. Which ones were the most meaningful to you? What have been your happiest moments? Look for the common threads. They might not be immediately obvious, but you will eventually see them.

2. Your Heroes

Who do you admire? Think of both the people you know personally and the people you don't. List both those living and those who have passed on. What do you admire about them? What character traits do they exemplify that you respect? Who is the one person who has made the greatest positive impact in your life?

The question is: What kind of person do you wish to become?

3. Your Big Result

What great result can you envision for your life? What would be a crowning accomplishment that you would be proud of having created or been known for? If some of the items on these lists don't seem to be directly related to your mission, they may very well be goals you want to achieve. So give yourself permission to dream.

4. Your Roles

List the various roles (community, family, career, etc.) you play and will likely play. How would you like to be described in each of these roles? What would you like your brother, daughter, boss, board member, spouse, etc. to say about you?

5. Document Your Aptitudes

List your skills and talents, your knowledge and expertise: things you are good at and that you enjoy doing. List your personal talents as well as your professional talents. Be sure to include those things you take for granted. They're important.

What are your greatest strengths?

What strengths have others, who know you well, noticed in you?

When you look at your work life, what activities do you consider of greatest worth?

When you look at your personal life, what activities do you consider of greatest worth?

What are the most important principles upon which your being and doing are based?

6. Your Goals: Dream Big

I'm a big advocate for keeping a list of everything you've ever wanted. If you don't have one, I recommend you start yours now because it will help you understand more of the direction in your life.

These are just *candidates* for goals. You're not committing to them. There's plenty of time to sort them out later. This is just the dreaming stage.

7. Your Service

Ultimately, your Meaningful Mission is the answer to this question: Who and how will I best serve?

The great Muhammad Ali said, "Service to others is the rent you pay for your room here on earth."

Michael E. Angier

> *"Service to others is the rent you pay for your room here on earth."*
> —Muhammad Ali

I believe you are uniquely qualified and compelled to serve in your own special way. Of the billions of people who have lived, there has never been another exactly you. Not a single one. You *do* have a mission. And right now, your mission is to create that mission.

8. Unlimited Thinking

One of the things I did to help me determine my Meaningful Mission was to do a fantasy exercise. I asked myself what would I do if I won a large lottery—say 50 million or more. After I bought all the toys, built the dream house, travelled about, what would I choose to do? I wanted to remove all the money and play distractions and focus on my calling. If I didn't need to work and could anything I wanted to do, *what would I do?*

I highly recommend it. It's fun and it's insightful. You will most likely learn a lot more about yourself and your motivations. And it just might uncover your true calling. It got me to do work that I would do for nothing. I've been doing work I love for nearly 40 years, and it has been financially rewarding as well.

9. Start Writing

Now that you've gone through these exercises, you're ready to create the first draft of your Meaningful Mission statement. Remember that you're not writing it for anybody but yourself, so write it in your own language.

Keep this question in mind as you write your draft: "Does this statement inspire the best in me?" Carry this draft with you and make notes and revisions before you attempt a second draft.

Once you've formed a permanent statement, review it frequently. To keep your vision and your values clearly in mind, memorize your statement. Post it where you'll see it daily. This helps strengthen your commitment.

Another Tool

Nightingale Conant has a free Personal Mission Statement Builder that you may find helpful in creating or refining (see Chapter 7) your mission statement. It promises a 5-minute solution, but you may find it useful.

www.Nightingale.com/personal-mission-statement

Michael E. Angier

Chapter 6:
Mission Statement Examples

> *"The longest journey is the journey inward."*
> —Dag Hammarskjöld

The following examples are just that, examples. They are not meant to be copied. Doing so will rob you of your unique and full potential. Use them for ideas on direction, result, who and how serviced, style, etc. I've included some corporate and organizational mission statements as well.

I'm not saying these are the best or that these even exemplify great mission statements. Some of them may have even changed, and I cannot vouch for their accuracy.

But they should give you some great ideas.

My mission in life is not merely to survive, but to thrive; and to do so with some passion, some compassion, some humor and some style.
—Maya Angelou

Michael E. Angier

To have fun in [my] journey through life and learn from [my] mistakes.

—Sir Richard Branson

To be the preeminent global hospitality company—the first choice of guests, team members, and owners alike.

—Hilton Hotels

To be a teacher. And to be known for inspiring my students to be more than they thought they could be.

—Oprah Winfrey

To be a loving teacher of simple truths to help myself and others to awaken the presence of God in their lives.

—Ken Blanchard, author

My passion is to take ideas that are of tremendous value and deliver them to a mass number of people in an impactful way. By utilizing new technology (software) and existing resources (motivational quotes) we can touch more people and help them experience an increase in the quality of life.

—Scott Geisel, president of *A New Life to Live*

Google's mission is to organize the world's information and make it universally accessible and useful.

—Google

How to Create Your Meaningful Mission

Our mission and values are to help people and businesses throughout the world realize their full potential.
—Microsoft

To help people and companies grow and prosper.
—Success Networks International

The Home Depot is in the home improvement business and our goal is to provide the highest level of service, the broadest selection of products and the most competitive prices.
—Home Depot

To teach, inspire, and empower myself and others, to create and live our best lives.
—Michael E. Angier

Serve Christ by ministering to the poor, the dying, and the hopelessly ill wherever the needy cried out for help.
—Mother Teresa

We save people money so they can live better. If we work together, we'll lower the cost of living for everyone…we'll give the world an opportunity to see what it's like to save and have a better life.
—Walmart

Michael E. Angier

Our mission is dedication to the highest quality of Customer Service delivered with a sense of warmth, friendliness, individual pride, and Company Spirit.

—Southwest Airlines

Our mission is to enable economic growth through infrastructure and energy development, and to provide solutions that support communities and protect the planet.

—Caterpillar, Inc.

We grant the wishes of children with life-threatening medical conditions to enrich the human experience with hope, strength and joy.

—Make-A-Wish® Foundation

Chapter 7:
Refining Your Mission Statement

> *"The whole of science is nothing more than a refinement of everyday thinking."*
> —Albert Einstein

Congratulations on creating your Meaningful Mission statement.

It's possible, but highly unlikely, that you've written your Meaningful Mission perfectly and it will stand as it is from this point forward.

Most likely you'll find ways to refine it so it has more clarity and meaning. Creating a clear, complete and concise statement may require several iterations.

That's why you don't want to do what so many others have done. And that is to file it away, consider it a job done and be through with it.

Your Meaningful Mission should be very much in the forefront of your mind. Test it. Make sure it fits. Make sure it inspires. Make sure it's big enough. Make sure it truly does have real meaning for you.

Michael E. Angier

Action Step

Look for ways to make your Meaningful Mission more succinct, clearer, more encompassing, shorter and more memorable.

Chapter 8:
Organizational Mission Statements

"If you don't know where you're going, how will you know when you're lost?"

In an entrepreneurial company, the owner(s) usually have a good sense of the direction, principles and goals for their organization. However, circumstances may find them becoming reactive to solve crises instead of paying attention to the important priorities that move their company toward its mission. They lose sight of their purpose.

The best organizational mission statement talks about the philosophies that will guide what the company is doing. It's an important tool to get everyone to pull together in the same direction. The key to a successful organizational mission statement is the process of participation. Everyone should participate in a meaningful way—not just the top management. Without involvement, there is no sense of commitment. Stephen Covey wrote, "An organizational mission statement—one that truly reflects the deep shared vision and values of everyone within that organization—creates a great unity and tremendous commitment. It creates in people's hearts and minds a frame of reference, a set of criteria or guidelines, by which they will govern themselves."

The organizational mission statement is similar to the personal mission statement in that it should address our basic human needs:

- financial or money need
- social or relationship need
- psychological or growth need
- spiritual or contribution need

And like the personal mission statement, it cannot be created overnight. It takes patience, a long-term perspective and involvement.

Clients/Customers

Some general questions include defining your commitment to several areas of your business.

Are you committed to providing high-quality service?

Are you fair, honest, courteous and professional in your business dealings?

Are you sensitive to your clients'/customers' needs and dedicated to their satisfaction?

Employees

Do you recognize the importance of each individual and his or her active role in the success of the entire company?

Do you provide your people opportunities to grow and feel motivated in their accomplishments?

Do you encourage the flow of communication and exchange of ideas through all levels of the company?

Industry

Are you committed to engaging in honest, lawful and professional business practices within your industry?

Do you respect the related industries that contribute to your success?

Are you committed to providing growth to your industry?

How do you distinguish your business from your competitors?

Community

Are you committed to the enhancement of the community of which you are a part?

Do you contribute to its economic vitality and consider the environmental impact of your growth?

Are you a symbol of leadership and active participation in community affairs?

These are the major categories to consider when developing an organizational mission statement. They could be subdivided into more distinct areas, depending on your business type, size and goals.

Some companies even break their mission statements into departmental creeds that remain connected to the main company mission statement.

Many organizations have a mission statement, but it doesn't benefit from the shared vision and commitment of its employees. When enhancing the existing mission statement, consider these key questions:

How many of the employees know that a company mission statement exists?

How many were involved in creating it?

How many really buy into it and use it as a frame of reference in making decisions?

Once these questions are answered, the organizational mission statement creates a great unity and deep sense of commitment. People are motivated by the same set of guidelines, creating a feeling of pride and satisfaction in their work.

And keep in mind that your mission statement can change as conditions change in the industry, economy or under a new management style.

Constant evaluation of the company's principles and beliefs keeps the mission statement in alignment with the changing value systems. It also creates a dynamic atmosphere of growth and change—without the degree of fear that change can produce.

And when people are totally involved in and committed to the evolution of the mission statement, they are swept up in the change and clearly understand the reasons why a new direction is needed.

Action Step

If you own a business or lead an organization, you should have a living, breathing Meaningful Mission statement for it. And if you're part of an organization that doesn't have a mission statement, I encourage you to utilize your knowledge and convictions to have one created.

Michael E. Angier

How to Create Your Meaningful Mission

Chapter 9:
Other Mission Statements

> *"Imagination is everything. It is the preview of life's coming attractions."*
> —Albert Einstein

When I was raising my children, we did not have a mission statement for our family. If I were to do it again, I would. If it's good for your life, if it's good for your business, why not a mission statement for your family? For your primary relationship?

And once you see how powerful and inspiring a Meaningful Mission is for your life, I'm convinced you will want one for your family as well.

My wife and I (we've been married for almost 25 years) have a mission statement to help guide our relationship. I share it with you, not as a model but as an example.

The mission of our marriage is to love, honor, support, nurture and care for one another. Our intention is to bring out the best in each other. We do this by trusting and being trustworthy. We do this with honesty and truthfulness. We are compassionate with each other. We back each other up and have each other's back. We ask for what we

Michael E. Angier

want and we do our best to fulfill each other's needs. We keep no secrets. When needed, we practice carefrontation (confronting issues and challenges in a caring fashion).

Committees, boards, home owner's associations, political parties, virtually any group, can benefit from a well-conceived and creative Mission Statement. It's always helpful to measure what's going on against the original mission. And it really helps to keep things from going astray.

Action Step

I urge you to create a mission statement for your family. The simple process of discussing what your mission statement would be will, in all likelihood, generate some good questions and enable you to be closer and more supportive of one another.

Chapter 10:
Overcoming Challenges to Your Mission

> *"That which can be foreseen can be prevented."*
> —Charles H. Mayo

I think it's important to know the pitfalls, the distractions and the enemies of creating and living your Meaningful Mission. In knowing them, you are better equipped to fight them off or avoid them altogether.

Here's what I see as the most common challenges to creating and living your Meaningful Mission.

Thinking Too Small

Small objectives are easier to believe in, but they lack motivation. A small goal says you can have me any time you want. But "any time" often becomes "no time" because it's insufficiently inspiring. What's easy to do is easy *not* to do.

Make sure your Meaningful Mission is big enough and worthy enough of your best efforts. Otherwise you will be cheating yourself—big time!

Lack of Belief

You have to believe in yourself, in your purpose, your mission, your vision—and in the power of this whole process.

Creating your Meaningful Mission using the strategies and tactics I've shared with you is not theoretical. These strategies have worked for many people, and they will work for you.

Invisible Mission

One of the things that will take you off track is not keeping your Meaningful Mission front and center in your life. Out of sight is very often out of mind.

Review it often. Keep reminders of the various aspects of your mission. See The Best Life Navigator below.

But bear in mind that forgetting about your Meaningful Mission *can* happen. Life gets busy and you can easily find yourself majoring in minor things.

Avoid the Nay' Sayers

Not everyone you encounter is going to be supportive and encouraging about your Meaningful Mission.

Be very careful who you share it with because even well-intentioned people can throw cold water on your dreams—oftentimes in the name of being *"realistic"*. If you're serious about living a big life, you can't spend time with small-thinking people. You can't talk "Butterfly" with "Caterpillar" people. You simply can't afford it.

Best Life Navigator

I created a template for Microsoft OneNote as a way to keep all my personal development, ideas, goals, core values, purpose, mission and vision statements, etc., all in one place—and much more.

How to Create Your Meaningful Mission

It's called The Best Life Navigator™ and it pulls everything together quite nicely. It's like a dashboard for living your best life. The Best Life Navigator will keep you much more organized, focused and directed.

And as a reader of this book, you get 50% off the current price when you use the coupon code MISSION. It comes with three valuable bonuses that I'm sure you will find useful. You can find out all about it at . . .

www.BestLifeNavigator.com

The main thing to keep in mind is to have your Meaningful Mission be a constant and uplifting reminder of the life you are choosing to live—and the reason for doing so.

Michael E. Angier

Chapter 11:
The Path to Your Best Life

*"To succeed in your mission,
you must have single-minded
devotion to your goal."*
—A. P. J. Abdul Kalam

As you saw from the Path to Your Best Life graphic in Chapter One, there are three other foundational aspects to living your Best Life.

They are your Core Values, your Purpose and your Vision.

I've written three more books in this series to address each of these very important topics (see *Other Books by Michael Angier* at the end of this book).

The reason is that your Meaningful Mission will be better and more complete if you are clear on your core values, your purpose and your vision for your life.

John Maxwell said, "Your core values are the deeply held beliefs that authentically describe your soul." And Stephen Covey said, "How different our lives are when we really know what is deeply important to us, and, keeping that picture in mind, we manage ourselves each day to be and to know what really matters most."

I believe in the wisdom both of these wise men.

Michael E. Angier

And at www.YourCoreValues.com, I share the *Top Ten Reasons to Know and Live Your Core Values*.

Also on that site, you get discounted access to a home-study course that goes in-depth into how to discover, document, articulate and live your core values. It's also available in a video course as part of the home-study course at no additional cost.

Action Step

Please give serious consideration to the Your Core Values course. It's nominally priced, a small investment for a great return. And it's really the foundation of the Best Life Path.

Chapter 12:
In Summary

> *"Here's the test to find whether your mission on Earth is finished: If you're alive, it isn't."*
> —Richard Bach

As important as having a clear and Meaningful Mission for your life is, I also believe you should enjoy the journey. You can and should be happy as you construct this beautiful life of yours—even when it's trying and challenging.

I love what my mentor Jim Rohn had to say about this: "Learn how to be happy with what you have, while you pursue all that you want."

> *"Learn how to be happy with what you have, while you pursue all that you want."*
> —Jim Rohn

One more word about not getting too quickly involved in the *how* of delivering on your Meaningful Mission. Getting too attached to the *way* your Mission will play out limits the manner in which it will be achieved. Focus on the results, not just the path.

How Did We Do?

I began planning and writing this book with several objectives:

> 1. Convince you of the value and the wisdom of investing in creating a Meaningful Mission for your life.
>
> 2. Help you to think bigger and believe in the possibilities of living up to your full and unique potential.
>
> 3. Encourage you to believe more in yourself, in this process and in what's possible.
>
> 4. Share resources and recommendations that will help you to create a clear and Meaningful Mission as a vehicle for living your Best Life.
>
> 5. Help you to dig deeper, think more comprehensively and eventually live in a more balanced, meaningful and significant fashion.

I hope we've been able to accomplish this together.

And if your Meaningful Mission is not yet clear to you, then that's your mission for now—to create your Meaningful Mission.

I wish for you to know your Empowering Purpose, have a Meaningful Mission, live your Vivid Vision, accomplish

How to Create Your Meaningful Mission

great things and feel the happiness, fulfillment and satisfaction that comes from a life well lived.

You can do it! You deserve it!

Have fun!

Michael E. Angier

A Thank You and a Request

Thank you for reading my book! I really appreciate all of your feedback, and I love hearing what you have to say.

I need your input to make the next version of this book—and my future books—better.

Please leave a brief and helpful review on Amazon to let me know what you thought of the book. Only about one in a thousand readers leave a review. I hope you will be a one-in-a-thousand reader.

You can use this link:
www.SuccessNet.org/go/amz-author

Thank you very much.

Michael E. Angier

BeYourBest@SuccessNet.org
www.SuccessNet.org

About the Author

Michael E. Angier is the founder and CIO (Chief Inspiration Officer) of SuccessNet based in the Tampa Bay area of Florida. He's a father, grandfather, husband, writer, speaker, entrepreneur, coach and student.

He's the author of the *101 Best Ways series, The Achievement Code, The Secret to Being Fiercely Focused, How to Create a Vivid Vision for Your Life, Discovering Your Empowering Purpose* and others.

Michael's work has been featured in numerous publications such as *USA Today, Selling Power, Personal Excellence* and *Sales & Marketing Excellence* as well as dozens of electronic publications. He's been interviewed on both TV and radio many times.

And his internationally popular articles have earned him a Paul Harris Fellowship with Rotary International.

Angier has experienced personal and professional success, but he's also suffered some bitter defeats. Although certainly preferring the former, he feels that he's learned the most from his struggles and disappointments. He feels that life's greatest lessons are learned by overcoming the

Michael E. Angier

obstacles in the path of a challenging and worthwhile objective.

Michael's passion is human potential. He believes fervently in the indomitable human spirit and revels in helping people and companies grow and prosper.

Over the past 40 years, Michael has devoted himself to studying what works and has been an ardent student of the principles of success. He's taught seminars and conducted workshops on goal setting, motivation and personal development in six countries.

Michael feels that there are three things essential to living a fulfilling and successful life: a purpose to live for, a self to live with and a faith to live by.

Michael is married to Dawn Angier—his partner, best friend, mentor, teacher, student and confidante. They have six adult children and five grandchildren. Michael enjoys tennis, reading, writing, publishing and helping people realize their dreams.

How to Create Your Meaningful Mission

Mistakes Happen

We're committed to publishing inspiring, practical and professional books. However, mistakes do occur. If you should find a typographical, grammatical or factual error, we would be most grateful if you let us know. And, if you are the first to tell us about it, we'd be happy to send you a thank you gift.

Just email your find with the book name, location and type of error to BeYourBest@SuccessNet.org with "Found This!" in the subject. Thanks for your help.

Michael E. Angier

Other Books by Michael Angier
www.Amazon.com/author/michaelangier

The Achievement Code
The 3C Formula for Getting What You Truly Want

The Achievement Code offers a simple, but proven, formula for getting what you truly want. With the Three C's, the author has distilled down from both ancient and modern teachers the true alchemy of success and achievement.

Whether they realized it or not, every single person who has ever achieved great things has employed the Three-C Formula. But not until Angier identified the Three Cs did the formula reveal itself. *The Achievement Code* outlines in simple, straightforward steps how to practice Clarity, Concentration and Consistency and actually get what you really want. Best-selling author, Bob Burg, writes in the Foreword, "It contains the basic principles of success upon which Michael has built his own ultra-successful life and business and upon which anyone else can do the same. In these teachings, he lays the foundation from which anyone can decide on a certain goal and by the very nature of the instruction provided, go about achieving it. In fact, if one will follow all three of the "C's" he teaches us, I cannot see how it would be possible not to succeed."

Other Books by Michael Angier

www.Amazon.com/author/michaelangier

Discover Your Empowering Purpose

Live Your Life with More Meaning, Significance and Fulfillment

Mark Twain claimed, "The two most important days in your life are the day you're born and the day you find out why."

The existential question, "Why am I here?" does have an answer. You have an Empowering Purpose for your life. You only need to discover and uncover what it is.

This book helps you do that. And in doing so, you can live with more meaning, significance and fulfillment. You will have more confidence, exhibit more courage and have more commitment because you are fulfilling your purpose.

The author leads you by the hand as you determine your unique and special abilities and eventually your particular Zone of Genius.

Knowing and understanding your Empowering Purpose is a true game changer. If you're looking for more direction, inspiration, motivation, determination and devotion, read this book, go through the exercises and watch your life catch on fire.

Michael E. Angier

Other Books by Michael Angier
www.Amazon.com/author/michaelangier

The Secret to Being Fiercely Focused

How to Have More Energy, Less Stress and
Get More Done by Tackling Your Tolerations

Are You Ready to Declutter Your Mind?

The Life-Changing Magic of Tidying Up: The Japanese Art of Decluttering and Organizing, has been off and on the New York Times Best Seller list for years—mostly on. If decluttering your home and office is life-changing, what about decluttering your *mind?*

Hundreds of thousands of books have been written on success—about what you need to get ahead. But what isn't talked about much is *what you need to get rid of.*

These niggly, spirit-sucking, energy-draining, peace-killers steal—often quite without detection—our joy, our happiness, our energy and our focus.

They are called Tolerations—things we tolerate, but shouldn't. And like weeds in a garden, we must recognize them for what they are and hoe them out—or they will take over our garden (life).

Other Books by Michael Angier

www.Amazon.com/author/michaelangier

Do You Have a Clear Vision for Your Life?

How to Create a Vivid Vision for Your Life gives you the impetus, the tools and the guidelines to create a meaningful, inspiring and detailed vision for your best life.

The author takes you by the hand and helps you dream big, think big and act even bigger.

This book will help you to . . .

- create a clear picture of the life you wish to create
- have more clarity and direction
- make better decisions and make them more easily
- have a bigger, better life
- have more balance in your life
- always know where you're going and what you want to achieve
- have more meaning and significance
- be more inspired, focused and motivated
- have more happiness by living on your terms

Don't let another day go by without creating a Vivid Vision for your life. Get your copy of this book now and make the rest of your life the best of your life.

Free Resources

Personal Achievement Assessment

Download this free tool from SuccessNet. With it, you'll be able to evaluate yourself in many different areas of your life and find even more ideas for living your Empowering Purpose. Consider it your personal success inventory (PDF format).
www.SuccessNet.org/psa

Subscribe to SuccessNet.org at No Cost

If you would like to be part of SuccessNet, you can subscribe for free at www.SuccessNet.org

We offer a valuable gift like a book, special report or eCourse (it changes regularly) to anyone who joins our mailing list. And three to five times a month, you will receive an article from Michael on a topic in support of living your best life. And there are hundreds of articles, resources, recordings and more available on the website.

You can also follow SuccessNet on Facebook at www.Facebook.com/ILikeSuccessNet or Michael's personal page at www.Facebook.com/michaelangier

Acknowledgements

I am truly grateful for my wife, Dawn, who is my business and life partner as well as my best friend. She provided not only encouragement and feedback, but also her highly professional copy editing and technical expertise. She always makes me—and my work—look better.

In addition, I wish to thank the tens of thousands of subscribers and members of SuccessNet.org, who over the past 24 years, have followed me and supported our efforts in helping us all create and live our Best Lives.

You are a great source of inspiration to me. And your patronage has allowed me to do work that I love for over two decades.

Made in the USA
Columbia, SC
01 January 2020